The Wolf

In a far northern land
the snow is melting,
and it will soon be spring.
Some wolves are lying in the sun.
A male wolf leaps up on a rock,
and looks out over the empty plain.
He pricks up his ears and sniffs the air.
He is Fang, the leader of the pack.

There are eight members of this small wolf pack:
five males and three she-wolves.
One of the she-wolves is not out in the sun.
She is hiding in an old fox-hole,
where she is caring for her three new cubs.
The other wolves dare not enter her den,
not even Fang, the father of the cubs.

Now Fang is ready to go.
He stretches his long legs, and yawns.
Can you see the four fang-like teeth?
The other wolves have been waiting for this moment.
It is time for the hunt to begin.

The wolves are excited and restless.
They wag their tails and sniff noses.
The other wolves greet Fang
with tails and bodies kept low,
and ears flattened to their heads.
They show him in all the ways they can
that he is their powerful leader,
and they will follow and obey.
Fang greets them with his tail up.
He is ready to lead the hunt.

Fang trots off across the snowy plain.
The rest of the pack follow in his tracks.
The mother-wolf stays behind, to look after her cubs.
In the distance, a herd of reindeer
is grazing among the melting snow.
Fang does not try to attack them.
He has learned in many hard winter hunts
that a wolf is no match for a healthy reindeer.
He prefers to track down animals which are sick,
or wounded, or young and helpless.

Fang sees an old lame elk
which is dragging its back leg.
The wolves begin to stalk the elk.
They spread out in a circle round it.
They try to get as close as possible
without alarming the elk.

The elk senses the danger, and runs limping away.
But it is too slow for a pack of hunting wolves.
Fang leaps at its nose, but is shaken off.
The rest of the pack attack the elk from all sides.
Within a few minutes, it is dead and partly eaten.

The she-wolf leaves the den for a few minutes
to go and drink from a nearby stream.
When she returns, she notices a strange scent.
A huge brown bear is prowling round her den.
He is sniffing for the remains of meat and bones
which the wolves have buried near the den.
The she-wolf snaps and snarls at the bear.
She is fearless in protecting her cubs,
and she will defend them to the death.

The wolves have eaten their fill of the dead elk.
They will not need to hunt again for several days.
As they are returning to the den,
Fang hears the mother-wolf snarling in the distance.
The wolves hurry back and surround the bear.
He knocks one wolf down with a blow of his paw,
but the others manage to drive him away.
That night the mother carries her cubs to a safer den.

The wolf-cubs are now two months old.
Their mother goes hunting with the pack once more.
One of the wolves, either an aunt or an uncle,
stays behind to baby-sit with the cubs.
When the older wolves return from a successful hunt
the cubs nudge at their mouths, asking for food.
The wolves bring up the warm meat from their stomachs.
This meat is easy for the cubs to eat and digest.
In this way, the cubs get plenty of food
to help them to grow big and strong before the winter.
All day they play and fight outside the den.
They test their strength against each other
to find out who will be leader when they grow up.

It is a day in late summer.
Before they hunt, the wolves
greet Fang as their leader.
Then the pack begins to howl.
Other wolf-packs hear the call.
They know this means they must
keep away from Fang's territory.

All summer, while the cubs were growing,
the wolf-pack stayed in the same part of the plain.
Now the cubs are big enough to move with the pack.
Soon the wolves will become wanderers,
following the reindeer herds to winter pastures
hundreds of kilometres away across the snow.

Some facts about wolves

At one time, wolves were found
all over Europe and North America.
But now they have been driven back
to wild places where few men live.
Unlike the fox, who hunts alone,
wolves prefer to live in packs.
Wolves live for about seven years.
They are trapped and shot by men
for their fur, and also because
they sometimes kill sheep and cows.
The wolf and the tame domestic dog
are closely related to each other.
Dogs are able to mate with wolves,
but not with foxes, jackals, coyotes,
and other members of the 'dog' family.
The dog who obeys his human master
is obeying his own 'pack-leader'.
The dog who becomes very excited
when his master gets ready for a walk
is acting in the same sort of way
as wolves behave before they hunt.
Dogs who are not kept under control
by their masters, can become wild,
and wander about in dog-packs.
We know many tales of wicked wolves.
But the wolf is really a timid animal,
who keeps away from his enemy, man.

Timber wolf

Tundra wolf

Red wolf

Coyote

Alsatian (or German shepherd dog)